STARTING ON JAN. 1, 2011, President Obama's economic recovery policy will begin the implementation of comprehensive, across-the-board tax rate increases for every major federal tax. The top two income tax rates will effectively climb by nearly 20 percent, counting the phaseout of deductions and exemptions. The top capital gains tax rate is scheduled to soar by nearly 60 percent, counting the application of ObamaCare's new 3.8 percent tax on investment income. The tax rate on dividends is scheduled to nearly triple, from 15 percent to 43.4 percent, counting the ObamaCare tax as well. The ObamaCare legislation also increased the top Medicare HI payroll tax rate by 31 percent. On our current course, the death tax will also be reimposed next year with a 55 percent top rate.

Meanwhile, America suffers under the second-highest – soon to be the highest – corporate tax rate in the industrialized world. The federal corporate tax rate of 35 percent is pushed close to 40 percent on average by

state corporate income taxes, leaving American businesses and employers uncompetitive in the global economy. Yet the Obama administration refuses to consider any reductions in this corporate tax rate.

Starting on Jan. 1, 2011, President Obama's economic recovery policy will begin the implementation of comprehensive, across-the-board tax rate increases for every major federal tax.

Ironically, however, much of the rest of the world has learned the lessons of Reaganomics. The average corporate tax rate in the European Union has been slashed from 38 percent in 1996 to 24 percent today. Germany's corporate tax rate has been reduced all the way to 15 percent, with Canada, now at 18 percent, scheduled to join them at 15 percent in 2012. Ireland adopted a corporate tax rate of 12.5 percent in 1988, which caused per capita income in that longtime poor country to soar from the second lowest in the EU to the second highest. Our own Department of the Treasury has said Ireland raises more corporate tax revenue as a percentage of gross domestic product than we do with our much higher rates. Corporate tax rates in India and China, our emerging competitors, are lower as well.

Instead of lowering these stifling business taxes, President Obama and congressional Democrats are increasing them. President Obama insists on double taxing the foreign earnings of American companies with a $122 billion tax increase, further reducing the international competitiveness of American businesses. Then there's a $90 billion tax increase on banks and a $40 billion increase on oil, gas, and coal producers.

ObamaCare adds still more tax increases.

A so-called "Cadillac" tax is imposed on high-value health plans equal to 40 percent of plan costs above certain thresholds, amounting to $32 billion in taxes on such health insurance during the first 10 years. But the thresholds are indexed only for general inflation, not health care inflation, so the tax will apply to more and more plans over time, eventually applying to average, ordinary plans. Less well known is that ObamaCare imposes a second tax on health insurance equal to $60 billion during the first 10 years. The health care takeover legislation also adopts new taxes on medical device manufacturers, prescription drugs, and even tanning salons, among other taxes.

The individual mandate requiring individuals without employer-provided health insurance to buy government-specified health insurance is also a tax. Even with the budget-crushing health insurance subsidies provided in the ObamaCare legislation, the required insurance will be quite expensive, ranging up to 2 percent of income for people at 133 percent of the poverty level and up to 9.8 percent for those at 400 percent of the poverty level ($88,000 for a family of four). That is like a new payroll tax.

The employer mandate in the ObamaCare legislation is also an economically deadly tax. For companies that do not currently provide health insurance to their employees, mostly smaller businesses, the employer mandate will add substantially to worker costs, killing jobs. In addition, in my own recently released comprehensive study of the ObamaCare legislation, *The ObamaCare Disaster: An Appraisal of the Patient Protection and Affordability Act*, published by The Heartland Institute, I explain all the ways in which the legislation will increase the cost of health insurance. With the employer mandate, this will kill jobs even for employers that currently provide health insurance, as their employee costs will also rise as a result.

But even with this already enacted tax tsunami, President Obama and congressional Democrats are *still* not satisfied. The cap-and-trade tax legislation was already passed in the House, with President Obama and Senate

Majority Leader Harry Reid supporting passage in the Senate. That legislation would require the purchase of permits for CO_2 emissions resulting from use of oil, natural gas, coal and any other cause. The number of permits would be limited and then reduced over the years to control and then reduce the total level of CO_2 emissions, making the available permits more and more expensive to purchase over time.

The legislation is explicitly intended to raise the cost of energy so much that total CO_2 emissions would be reduced 17 percent by 2020 and 83 percent by 2050. That would take America back to the per capita CO_2 emission levels of the late 19th century, effectively repealing the Industrial Revolution, which arose based on the use of fossil fuels. Some politicians have ludicrously suggested this could be done at a cost to families of only a couple of dollars a week. But achieving those levels of reduction would require trillions of dollars in higher costs for at least the next several decades, with costs higher to the extent that the government keeps CO_2-free nuclear power under wraps.

Then there is President Obama's debt commission, working away to produce a report after the elections this fall. Among the top options is a new value-added tax (VAT), which would be incorporated in the price of every product and service in the economy. Speaker of the House Nancy Pelosi has already proclaimed her support for a VAT.

Tax Rates and Incentives

The key to understanding the impact of tax increases on the economy is to focus on tax rates, particularly the marginal tax rate, which is the tax rate that applies to the last dollar earned. The tax rate determines how much the producer is allowed to keep out of what he or she produces. For example, at a 25 percent tax rate, the producer keeps three-fourths of his production. If that rate is increased to 50 percent, the producer keeps only half of what he produces, reducing his reward for production and output by one-third. Incentives are consequently slashed for productive activity, such as savings, investment, work, business expansion, business creation, job creation, and entrepreneurship. The result is fewer jobs, lower wages, and slower economic growth, or even an economic downturn.

In contrast, if the tax rate is reduced from 50 percent to 25 percent, what producers are allowed to keep from their production increases from one-half to three-fourths, increasing the reward for production and output by one-half. That sharply increases incentives for all of the above productive activities, resulting in more of them, and more jobs, higher wages, and faster economic growth.

Moreover, these incentives do not just expand or contract the economy by the amount of any tax cut or tax increase. For example, a tax cut of $100 billion involving reduced tax rates does not just affect the economy by $100 billion. The lower tax rates affect every dollar and every economic decision throughout the economy. That is because every economic decision is based on the new lower tax rates. Indeed, the new lower tax rates affect every dollar, or unit of currency, and every economic decision throughout the whole world regarding whether to invest in America, start or expand businesses here, create jobs here, or even work here. All these decisions will be based on the new lower tax rates. Tax rate increases have just the opposite effect on every dollar and economic decision throughout the economy and the world.

Multiple Taxation of Capital

These incentive effects are compounded in our tax system through the multiple taxation of capital. Capital income is taxed not once, but several times in our system. For example, consider a saver who invests a dollar in a corporate enterprise. Any dollar that corporation earns is taxed at the corporate income tax rate, totaling roughly 40 percent in America on average now. If the remainder of that dollar is paid to the investor in dividends, then it is taxed again through the individual income tax at the dividends tax rate. With President Obama increasing the dividends tax rate from 15 percent to 43.4 percent, applying that 43.4 percent tax rate to the 60 cents remaining after paying the corporate income tax leaves just 34 cents for the investor out of the original dollar earned. Don't expect much job-creating investment as a result.

But there is more. A third layer of taxation of capital income is represented by the capital gains tax. Consider an asset such as a share of stock. When the price of that asset increases, that is reflecting an increase in the expected value of the future income stream. That future income will be taxed by both the corporate income tax and the individual income tax when earned. If that asset is sold now, taxing the increased value by the capital gains tax is effectively taxing that future income stream a third time.

The death tax is still another, fourth layer of taxation of capital income. If the investor in our example above saves the 34 cents re -

maining on that dollar of corporate earnings after paying the corporate and individual income tax and leaves it to his children at death, applying the death tax to it would take roughly half of what is left, leaving his children just 17 cents out of the original dollar earned.

Our tax system further burdens capital income through depreciation rather than immediate expensing. Except for capital investment in plants and equipment, all other business expenses are deducted in the year they are incurred, because the income tax is supposed to be on net income after expenses. But deductions for the expenses of acquiring capital equipment must be spread out over many years under arbitrary depreciation schedules. Capital equipment is what makes American workers the most productive, and hence the most highly paid with the highest standard of living, in the world. With such capital equipment, for example, workers can use mechanized, computerized, modern crane shovels rather than their bare hands for digging and building. Or they can use modern computers rather than just computing in their heads. The result of extended arbitrary depreciation schedules instead of immediate deductions or expensing is less of such capital equipment, slowing growth in jobs, productivity, and wages.

With President Obama and congressional Democrats increasing virtually all of these multiple layers of taxation on capital income, the interacting effects are compounded. That is why investing in America right now is like anchoring an unarmed cargo ship off the coast of Somalia. The natural result of the incentive effects of the tax increases is the capital flight and effective capital strike we are seeing in America right now. World capital, including capital from U.S. investors, is trending toward the more rapidly growing emerging economies and other economies recovering far faster and stronger than we are. That is the reason as well for American companies sitting on $2 trillion of capital right now and for banks sitting on a trillion dollars in excess reserves. The economy is poised to boom, and it can't wait to do so, but President Obama's tax piracy is barring the way.

President Obama's Tax Welfare

President Obama claims to have cut taxes for 95 percent of workers. But those "tax cuts" have all involved tax *credits* rather than reductions in tax *rates*. The centerpiece is a $400-per-year, $7.69-per-week "Making Work Pay" tax credit that is scheduled to expire soon.

Such tax credits do not work to stimulate economic growth, because they do not change the fundamental incentives that govern the economy. A $400 tax credit involves the government either explicitly or effectively sending you a check for $400. But after that, you and everyone else still face the same tax rates and economic incentives as before.

Tax cuts do not expand the economy by "putting more money in people's pockets," thereby leading to increased spending. Increased welfare benefits would put more money in people's pockets as well. But this is an outdated Keynesian rationale from the 1930s that does not work for two reasons. First, the government has to borrow or tax the money from someone else in the economy to give you the tax credit or increased welfare check. So, if it takes $400 out of the economy to give you $400 through the tax credit or increased welfare, it has not added anything to the economy on net. Second, again, there is no change in fundamental incentives.

Note also that Obama's tax credits are refundable, which means if you do not have enough income tax liability for the credit to offset, the government will send you a check for the difference. The tax credit in this case is entirely indistinguishable from welfare, which is never going to be the foundation for a booming economy. Obama's own budget documents show that 35 percent of his supposed income tax cuts go to people who do not pay income taxes; therefore, they are not tax cuts at all, but welfare checks. This is why Obama's own budget accounts for this portion of his supposed tax cuts as outlays rather than revenue reductions. You can't *cut* income taxes for people who do not pay income taxes.

Just Taxing the Rich?

President Obama's apologists argue that his tax increases only apply to "the rich" making more than $200,000 a year for singles and $250,000 a year for married couples. That affects only the top 2 percent of income earners and only 3 percent of small businesses, they contend. These rich "can afford" the tax increases, they say. They don't "need" the lower tax rates from the Bush tax cuts, which President Obama is going to let expire for them.

Note that except for the new 3.8 percent tax on investment and the Medicare payroll tax increase, all of the ObamaCare tax increases apply to those making less than $250,000 per year as well as to those making more than that arbitrary limit. This includes, most importantly, the individual mandate. Before passage of ObamaCare, President Obama argued on national TV that it would be ludicrous to consider the individual mandate a tax, regardless of what the dictionary says. After passage, his lawyers were in court arguing that the individual mandate is constitutionally justified because it is a tax. The cap-and-trade tax and the potential VAT also would apply to everyone, including those making less than $250,000 per year.

Moreover, as Kevin Hassett and Alan Viard explained in *The Wall Street Journal* on Sept. 3, 2010, "The 3% [of small businesses] figure ... is based on simply counting the number of tax returns with any pass-through business income. So, if somebody makes a little money selling products on eBay and reports that as income on Schedule C of their tax return, they are counted as a small business." Hassett and Viard explain the truly relevant data, saying,

> *According to IRS data, fully 48% of the net income of sole proprietorships, partnerships, and S corporations reported on tax returns went to households with incomes above $200,000 in 2007. That's the number to look at, not the 3%. Would Mrs. Pelosi and Mr. Biden deny that the*

more successful firms owned by individuals in the top income-tax bracket are disproportionally responsible for investment and job creation?

In other words, the tax increases directly affect half of all small-business income, not just 3 percent, and those more successful small businesses are responsible for an even larger share of the employment created.

Moreover, tax rate increases impact not only those currently in the affected tax brackets, but also those who expect or hope to be at those income levels in the future. An entrepreneur starting a small business may earn only $25,000 in the first year but may expect to make more than $250,000 once the business is successful, which is his incentive for starting the business in the first place. But higher tax rates that would depreciate the reward if he is successful may well stop him from even trying in the first place.

In addition, the venture capitalists and other investors essential for small businesses to succeed are directly affected by the higher tax rates, even if the small-business owner himself is not yet. Higher tax rates can and will prevent such small-business investments from ever occurring.

In the end, it is not about whether investors, entrepreneurs, or small businesses can "afford"

Through these economic effects, President Obama's comprehensive tax rate increases will harm everyone.

---

increased taxes or "need" any tax cuts, which is a neosocialist argument. It is about what effect the tax rate increases will have on the economy, jobs, revenues, the nation's standard of living, and other factors. Through these effects, President Obama's comprehensive tax rate increases will harm everyone.

* * *

While President Obama and his hypnotized acolytes do not understand any of this, President John F. Kennedy did. Kennedy proposed legislation to reduce income tax rates across the board by 30 percent. Kennedy explained,

> *It is a paradoxical truth that tax rates are too high today, and tax revenues are too low and the soundest way to raise the revenues in the long run is to cut the tax rates.... [A]n economy constrained by high tax rates will never produce enough revenue to balance the budget, just as it will never create enough jobs or enough profits.*

Kennedy added,

> *Our true choice is not between tax reduction, on the one hand, and the avoidance of large federal deficits on the other.... It is between two kinds of deficits – a chronic deficit of inertia, as the unwanted result of result of inadequate revenues and a restricted economy – or a temporary deficit*

of transition, resulting from a tax cut designed to boost the economy, produce revenues, and achieve a future budget surplus.

Kennedy explained further that the best way to promote economic growth "is to reduce the burden on private income and the deterrents to private initiative which are imposed by our present tax system – and this administration is pledged to an across-the-board reduction in personal and corporate income tax rates."

Kennedy's proposed tax rate cuts were adopted in 1964, cutting the top tax rate from 91 percent to 70 percent, as well as reducing the lower rates. The next year, economic growth soared by 50 percent, and *income tax revenues* ***increased*** *by 41 percent!* By 1966, unemployment had fallen to its lowest peacetime level in almost 40 years. *U.S. News & World Report* exclaimed, "The unusual budget spectacle of sharply rising revenues following the biggest tax cut in history is beginning to astonish even those who pushed hardest for tax cuts in the first place." Arthur Okun, the administration's chief economic adviser, estimated that the tax cuts expanded the economy in just two years by 10 percent above where it would have been.

In 1981, Reagan cut the top income tax rate of 70 percent to 50 percent, with a 25 percent across-the-board reduction in income tax rates for everyone else. Then, in the 1986 tax reform, he cut the top rate to 28 percent, with only one other rate of 15 percent for everyone else. Reagan also cut corporate income tax rates and, initially, capital gains rates as well.

By the end of 1982, just before the tax cuts were fully phased in, the economy took off on a 25-year boom, with just slight interruptions by shallow, short recessions in 1990 and 2001. As Arthur Laffer and Stephen Moore write in their book, *The End of Prosperity: How Higher Taxes Will Doom the Economy – If We Let It Happen*,

> *We call this period, 1982–2007, the twenty-five year boom – the greatest period of wealth creation in the history of the planet. In 1980, the net worth – assets minus liabilities – of all U.S. households and business ... was $25 trillion in today's*

dollars. By 2007 . . . net worth was just shy of $57 trillion. Adjusting for inflation, more wealth was created in America in the twenty-five year boom than in the previous two hundred years.

In 1984, the economy grew by 6.8 percent *in real terms*, the highest in 50 years. Nearly 20 million new jobs were created from 1983 to 1989, increasing U.S. civilian employment by almost 20 percent. Unemployment fell to 5.3 percent by 1989. Even with the Reagan tax cuts, total federal revenues doubled from 1980 to 1990, growing from $517.1 billion to $1,031 billion, or just more than $1 trillion. In Reagan's last budget year, fiscal year 1989, the widely overballyhooed federal deficit had declined to $152.5 billion, about the same as a percent of GDP as in 1980, 2.9 percent compared with 2.8 percent.

Contributing to the extension of this Reagan recovery into the 25-year boom were the tax cuts and other pro-growth policies adopted by the Newt Gingrich-led congressional majorities in the 1990s and the much-maligned George W. Bush tax cuts adopted in

2001 and 2003, which mostly followed in the steps of Kennedy and Reagan. Although the 2001 tax cut included some non-growth tax reductions, such as increasing the child tax credit, it also reduced the top marginal income tax rate from 39.6 percent to 35 percent, a reduction of only 11 percent that he had to fight for tooth and nail. Bush's 2001 tax cuts also reduced the rate for the lowest-income workers by 33 percent, from 15 percent down to 10 percent. In 2003, Bush cut the capital gains tax rate by 33 percent and the income tax rate on corporate dividends by more than half.

These tax rate cuts reversed the short, shallow 2001 recession and the negative economic effects of the Sept. 11, 2001, terrorist attacks, restoring growth. After the rate cuts were all fully implemented in 2003, the economy created 7.8 million new jobs, and the unemployment rate fell from more than 6 percent to 4.4 percent. Real economic growth during the next three years doubled from the average for the prior three years to 3.5 percent.

Business investment spending, which had declined for nine straight quarters, reversed and increased by 6.7 percent per quarter. Manufacturing output soared to its highest level in 20 years. The stock market revived, creating almost $7 trillion in new shareholder wealth. From 2003 to 2007, the S&P 500 almost doubled.

Capital gains tax revenues had *doubled* by 2005, *despite the 33 percent rate cut.* In the last budget adopted by a Republican-controlled Congress, for fiscal year 2007, the budget deficit was $161 billion, only a small fraction of President Obama's budget deficits. The argument of some Obama propagandists that the Bush tax rate cuts caused the 2008 financial crisis has the same intellectual grounding as Soviet-era agitprop.

As Laffer and Moore write regarding the economy by 2007, "The economy in real terms is almost twice as large today as it was in the late 1970s." Steve Forbes summarizes,

> *Between the early 1980s and 2007 we lived in an economic Golden Age. Never before have so*

many people advanced so far economically in so short a period of time as they have during the last 25 years. Until the credit crisis, 70 million people a year [worldwide] were joining the middle class. The U.S. kicked off this long boom with the economic reforms of Ronald Reagan, particularly his enormous income tax cuts. We burst from the economic stagnation of the 1970s into a dynamic, innovative, high-tech-oriented economy. Even in recent years the much maligned U.S. did well. Between year-end 2002 and year-end 2007 U.S. growth exceeded the entire size of China's economy.

In other words, the *growth* in the U.S. economy from 2002 to 2007 was the equivalent of adding the entire economy of China to the U.S. economy.

Peak Obama

Just as President Obama is following the opposite of President Reagan's economic policies in every detail, the result will be the opposite as well.

Instead of increasing spending with a trillion-dollar "stimulus" spending bill, Reagan came into office in 1981 with his much-derided budget cuts, cutting out close to 5 percent of federal spending right away. In constant dollars, nondefense discretionary spending declined by 14.4 percent from 1981 to 1982 and by 16.8 percent from 1981 to 1983. Moreover, in constant dollars, this nondefense discretionary spending never returned to its 1981 level for the rest of Reagan's two terms. By 1988, this spending was still down 14.4 percent from its 1981 level, in constant dollars.

Instead of the Fed madly gunning the money engines as today, Reagan's Fed pursued a historic tightening that wrung out the Great Inflation that had been accelerating at a frightening pace since 1968, with prices rising 25 percent during 1979 and 1980. The annual inflation had been cut in half by 1982 to 6.2 percent and in half again by 1983 to 3.2 percent, leaving inflation tamed for a generation thereafter.

Moreover, instead of President Obama's policy of mad reregulation, President Reagan pursued pathbreaking deregulation that ultimately saved consumers and the American economy trillions of dollars. Finally, as explained above in detail, while President Reagan enacted historic reductions in tax rates, President Obama is pursuing comprehensive, across-the-board tax rate increases for every major federal tax.

Reagan's second year was his rockiest in terms of overall economic performance, because wringing out such high inflation so rapidly stifled the economy, a result that any college economics textbook will explain. Moreover, his tax rate reductions were phased in and did not become fully effective until Jan. 1, 1983. Arthur Laffer has long argued that the phasing in affirmatively delayed economic growth.

In mirror image, this second year of President Obama, as bad as it is, will be the best of his reign of error, unless new congressional majorities reverse his policies. The economy this year has been benefiting from what economists call "the slingshot effect," the natural tendency of the economy to snap back as smartly as the downturn was steep. That results naturally because every day, businesses scramble to rebuild themselves and workers seek new and better employment. That is why it is called the business *cycle.* That is also why the average recession since World War II has lasted only 10 months, with the longest previously lasting 16 months. By next year, this slingshot effect will be stale, and the stimulative effect of any snapback from the steepness of the downturn will be spent.

The economy has also benefited this year from record-low interest rates of nearly zero and the Fed's enormously expansive monetary policy. But there is only one way for interest rates to go from here. (Note that in Reagan's second year, interest rates were in long-term decline from historic highs, portending the coming boom.)

The positive effect of the enormous Fed monetary expansion will also soon be petering out, if it hasn't already. Monetary expansion does not create long-term economic growth. The Fed has to press the accelerator faster and faster to maintain the same stimulative effect. But if it does, then inflation starts to rise, accelerating faster and faster if the Fed continues. Indeed, the runaway expansion of the monetary base the Fed has already engineered will generate explosive inflation if the Fed does not pull it out in time.

Laffer has also emphasized that the specter of the comprehensive tax rate increases starting in 2011, precisely the opposite of the Reagan term, is boosting the economy this year, as producers scramble to produce what they can this year before the grim reaper arrives next year.

Yet despite all these favorable factors, the economy has been surprisingly weak this year, stunted by the fallacies of Keynesian Obamanomics. While the average recession since World War II has lasted 10 months and the longest previously has been 16 months, the disastrous August jobs report shows that

32 months since the official start of the recession, scored by the National Bureau of Economic Research as beginning in December 2007, the economy is *still* losing jobs and un-employment is *still* rising. The Department of Labor reported another 54,000 jobs lost in August 2010, with unemployment rising to 9.6 percent. Major Obama voting blocs are being punished by Obamanomics. African Americans suffer a sustained depression reflected by 16.3 percent unemployment, and Hispanics are not far behind at 12 percent unemployment. It is even worse for teenagers, with unemployment at 26.3 percent.

The total army of the unemployed remains stuck at nearly 15 million, with 42 percent of those classified as long-term unemployed, jobless for more than six months, the highest since the Great Depression. The number of additional workers employed part time for economic reasons was still rising in August, up by another 331,000 to nearly 9 million. The Bureau of Labor Statistics (BLS) defines these workers as those who "were working part time because their hours had been cut back or because they were unable to find a full-time job."

Another 2.4 million were defined as marginally attached to the labor force, stuck at that total for a year. The BLS explains that these individuals "wanted and were available for work, and had looked for a job sometime in the prior 12 months," but were not counted among the unemployed because they had not looked for work in the prior four weeks. These included 1.1 million discouraged workers, up 352,000 over the past year, not currently searching for work and therefore not counted as unemployed, because they believe that in the economy of hope and change, no jobs are available for them.

The army of the unemployed and underemployed consequently stands at 26.2 million Americans. That would add up to an unemployed and underemployed rate of 16.7 percent almost three years after the recession started. The full picture of hopelessness is measured by the precipitous drop in the civilian-employment population ratio, from 63 percent in 2007 to 58 percent today, fully reflecting the millions who have dropped out of the workforce altogether, giving up.

Moreover, the economic growth we have experienced recently has been less than half the growth we experienced after similarly severe downturns. The economy grew by almost 7 percent in Reagan's recovery in 1983 and 1984. Even under President Ford, real GDP grew by 6.2 percent in the year after the 1974–75 recession.

The accompanying graphs show what to expect in the next two years if the performance of the economy under President Obama is to be the mirror-image reverse of the performance under President Reagan. This would be the natural, logical result of following the mirror-image opposite of Reagan's economic program, including the above-discussed incentive effects of Obama's comprehensive federal tax rate increases, the costs and burdens of Obama's reregulation hitting next year, and the continued drain of private-sector resources

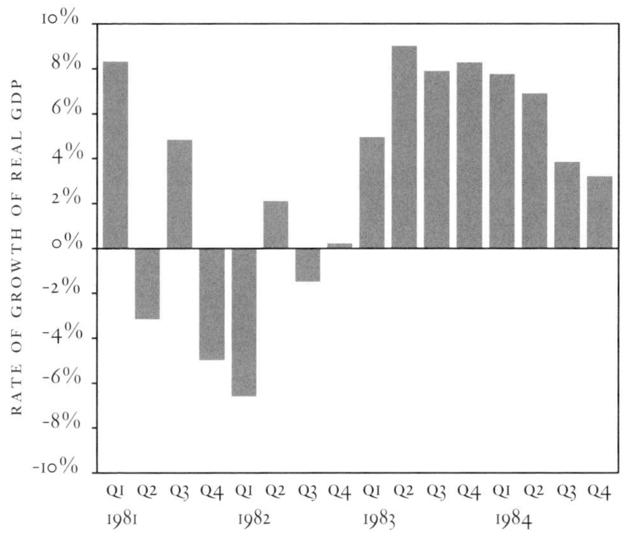

THE REAGAN RECOVERY

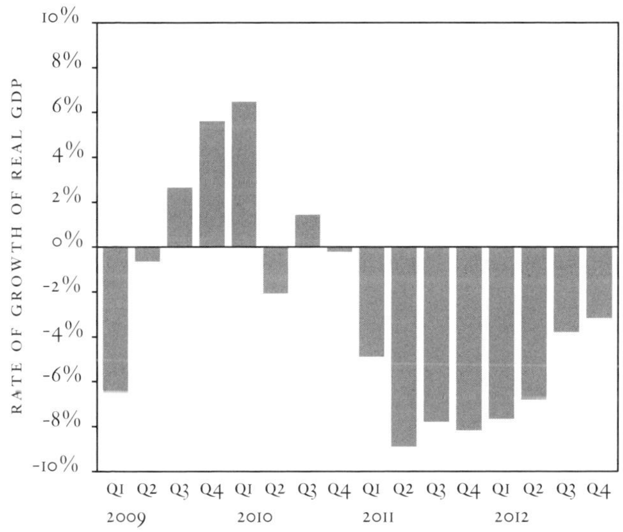

THE OBAMANOMICS RECOVERY
AS THE OPPOSITE OF REAGANOMICS

Economic growth is in a tailspin, falling from 5% in the fourth quarter of 2009 to 3.7% in the first quarter of 2010 to 1.6% in the second quarter.

---

caused by President Obama's supposedly stimulative spending increases and deficits. Laffer explains,

> *[W]hen the U.S. economy comes to 2011, the train's going to come off the tracks. . . . The tax boundary that will occur on January 1, 2011 tells me that* GDP *growth in 2010 will be some 6 percent to 8 percent higher than* GDP *growth in 2011. A year on year decline from trend of some 6 percent to 8 percent in* GDP *growth would represent a larger collapse than occurred in 2008 and early 2009.*

We see signs of that already even in this year's Peak Obama economy. Economic growth is in a tailspin, falling from 5 percent in the fourth quarter of 2009 to 3.7 percent in the first quarter of 2010 to 1.6 percent in the second quarter. Unemployment is rising again, with the economy continuing to lose jobs every month. The stock market is stalled, mired 30 percent below its record highs over 14,000 in the Dow. This weak economy couldn't be a worse time to raise federal tax rates across the board.

President Obama's Revenue Gap

President Obama's budget projects that his tax increases on "the rich" (singles making more than $200,000 and couples making more than $250,000) would raise $678 billion in increased revenue during the next 10 years. The ObamaCare legislation projected another $210 billion from the increased payroll taxes on those workers for a total of nearly $1 trillion. But these tax increases won't raise anywhere near the revenue projected. Obama will be lucky if this tax piracy doesn't result in *less* revenue.

For example, during the past 40 years,

every time capital gains tax rates have been cut, revenues have *increased*, and every time capital gains tax rates have been increased, revenues have *decreased*. In 1968, a 25 percent capital gains tax rate generated real capital gains tax revenues of $40.6 billion, calculated in 2000 dollars. The capital gains tax rate was then raised four times in the next seven years to 35 percent. By 1975, at the higher rate, capital gains revenues totaled $19.6 billion in constant 2000 dollars, less than half as much.

In 1978, the capital gains tax rate of 35 percent yielded $29.9 billion in 2000 dollars.

During the past 40 years, every time capital gains tax rates have been cut, revenues have increased, and every time capital gains tax rates have been increased, revenues have decreased.

The rate was then cut three times to 20 percent during the next four years. By 1986, the new rate, 43 percent lower than the 1978 rate, raised $92.9 billion in 2000 dollars, about three times as much. The capital gains rate was raised by 40 percent the next year, to 28 percent. Capital gains revenues fell to $56.2 billion that year and declined all the way to $34.6 billion by 1991.

In 1997, Congress cut the capital gains tax rate from 28 percent back down to 20 percent. Despite this almost 30 percent cut in the rate, capital gains revenues rose from $62 billion in 1996 to $109 billion in 1999. Revenues in the period of 1997 to 2000 increased by 84 percent over the projections before the tax cut.

Finally, Congress cut the capital gains rate from 20 percent to 15 percent in 2003. Capital gains revenues doubled from 2003 to 2005, despite this 33 percent cut in the rate. Revenues increased by $133 billion during the years from 2003 to 2006 as compared with pre-tax-cut projections.

President Obama's capital gains tax increases will only add to this historical record, resulting in less revenue rather than more.

Moreover, dividends paid soared after Bush cut the dividends tax in 2003, resulting in more revenue rather than less. President Obama's crushing dividends tax increase means that only 34 cents on average would be left out of a dollar of corporate earnings paid as dividends. That will result in a collapse in dividends paid, as corporations keep the cash to invest themselves, again resulting in less revenue rather than more.

The projections of higher revenues from the other tax rate increases all fail to take into account the negative incentive effects discussed above and the counterproductive interactions from all those effects. Since we know from experience that those incentive effects are powerful and real, the result at a minimum will be less revenue than expected, if not less revenue overall.

Even with all of Obama's tax increases and the increased revenue as projected, the CBO projects that by 2012, the national debt will have doubled in only four years to $11.5 trillion. By 2020, it will have almost quadrupled since 2008 to $20.3 trillion. By the end of this year, the CBO projects the national debt will reach 62 percent of GDP, higher than at any time in our history except for World War II and shortly thereafter. Indeed, as Brian Riedl of The Heritage Foundation reports, the national debt is rocketing upward so fast that under current policies, more debt will be run up under eight years of President Obama than under all other presidents in history – from George Washington to George W. Bush – combined.

But since all of the tax increases on "the rich" won't raise nearly the projected revenue, federal deficits and debt will be even higher than this. The Obama budget already projects that net interest spending will soar to $840 billion by 2020, more than four times the current levels. Less revenue than now expected means this interest spending is also going to be higher, which translates into even more deficits and debt. If interest rates rise higher than the modest levels the Obama budget now projects, all of this tailspins into an even worse downward spiral.

Finally, if President Obama's comprehensive tax rate increases go through next year as planned, the probability of another double-dip recession will be more than 100 percent, if not Arthur Laffer's Coming Crash of 2011. That will leave the federal government with much less revenue overall, rather than more. Where will that leave the current deficit of $1.5 trillion? Well more than $2 trillion, making a mockery of the very notion of a federal budget.

Tax Piracy

President Obama's apologists argue that his tax increases on "the rich" are necessary just so the rich will pay their fair share. But even before President Obama was elected, official IRS data showed that in 2007, the top 1 percent of income earners paid 40.4 percent of all federal income taxes, almost twice their share of adjusted gross income. The top 5 percent paid 60.6 percent of all federal income taxes while earning 37.7 percent of adjusted gross income. The top 10 percent paid 71.2 percent of all income taxes while earning 48 percent of adjusted gross income.

Meanwhile, the bottom 50 percent of income earners paid only 2.9 percent of all federal income taxes. Indeed, the bottom 95 percent of income earners paid 39.4 percent of all federal income taxes. That means the top 1 percent of income earners pay more federal income taxes than the bottom 95 percent!

This should lead you to ask regarding "the

Even before President Obama was elected, official IRS data showed that in 2007, the top 1% of income earners paid 40.4% of all federal income taxes.

---

rich," just what would be their "fair share"?

IRS data also show that those earning more than $200,000 a year, on whom President Obama wants to increase taxes, constitute just 3 percent of taxpayers. Yet that 3 percent pays more in income taxes than the bottom 97 percent combined.

Given these facts, those who want to increase taxes on the top 1 percent of income earners, or the top 3 percent, in the name of "fairness" profess the morality of pirates or of gang rape. Moreover, the notion that still more revenues can be reaped from this narrow slice of taxpayers is daft. This is where the capital flight and capital strike is coming from.

The facts also demonstrate the falsehood of the charge made by Obama and the Democrats that Republicans cut taxes for the rich but haven't "given a break to folks who make less." The share of income taxes paid by the highest-income earners has basically doubled since 1981, when President Reagan brought his supply-side economics to Washington. That is because with the lower tax rates, incomes boomed along with the economy, and high-income taxpayers had the incentives to pull their money out of tax shelters and invest it in the real economy, fueling the boom.

But in 2007, again before President Obama was even elected, the bottom 40 percent of income earners as a group paid no federal income taxes. Instead, they received net payments from the income tax system equal to 3.8 percent of all federal income taxes. In other words, they paid negative 3.8 percent of federal income taxes. The middle 20 percent of income earners, the actual middle class, paid 4.7 percent of all federal income taxes.

This is the result of Reagan Republican supply-side economics that began with Reagan and Jack Kemp in the 1970s and 1980s, continued through Newt Gingrich and his Contract with America, and further played out with the Bush tax cuts of 2001 and 2003. Reagan and his Republicans abolished federal income taxes on the poor and working class. Moreover, they almost abolished federal income taxes on the actual middle class (the middle 20 percent).

It was, in fact, Ronald Reagan who first proposed in the 1970s the Earned Income Tax Credit (EITC), his alternative to welfare, which has done so much to reduce income tax liabilities for lower-income people. As president, he cut federal income tax rates by 25 percent across the board for all taxpayers. He also indexed the tax brackets for all taxpayers to prevent inflation from pushing workers into higher tax brackets.

In the Tax Reform Act of 1986, he reduced the federal income tax rate for "folks who make less" all the way down to 15 percent. That act also doubled the personal exemption, shielding more income from taxation for everybody.

Newt Gingrich's Contract with America adopted a child tax credit of $500 per child that reduced the tax liabilities of lower-income people by a higher percentage than for higher-income people. President Bush doubled that credit to $1,000 per child and made it refundable so that low-income people who do not even pay $1,000 in federal income taxes could still get the full credit. Bush also adopted a new lower tax bracket of 10 percent for the lowest-income workers, reducing their federal income tax rate by 33 percent. Again,

---

Taxes as a percent of GDP *should be taken as a reverse indicator of economic freedom. Higher taxes as a percent of* GDP *mean less economic freedom; lower taxes as a percent of* GDP *mean more.*

---

he cut the top rate for the highest-income workers by just 11.6 percent, from 39.6 percent to 35 percent.

Many conservatives do not think it was a good idea to exempt so many from paying any income taxes at all. Nevertheless, the charge that the Republicans only cut taxes for the rich is factually groundless. Under Reagan Republican tax policies, the share of income taxes paid by the rich has soared to arguably excessive, even abusive levels, while income taxes were, again, abolished for the poor and working class and almost abolished for the middle class.

Taxes and Economic Freedom

Instead of judging taxes by the morality of tax piracy, the only reasonable way to judge taxes is by their impact on economic growth, prosperity, and economic freedom. Higher taxes mean less personal freedom, because they reduce personal control over your income, and the government rather than you decides how it is spent or saved. Lower taxes mean more personal freedom, because they increase personal control over your own income and leave you with more of your own income to choose to save, spend, or invest as you desire.

Therefore, taxes as a percent of GDP should be taken as a reverse indicator of economic freedom. Higher taxes as a percent of GDP mean less economic freedom; lower taxes as a percent of GDP mean more.

First American edition published in 2010 by Encounter Books, an activity of Encounter for Culture and Education, Inc., a nonprofit, tax exempt corporation.
Encounter Books website address: www.encounterbooks.com

Manufactured in the United States and printed on acid-free paper. The paper used in this publication meets the minimum requirements of ANSI/NISO Z39.48-1992 (R 1997) (*Permanence of Paper*).

FIRST AMERICAN EDITION

LIBRARY OF CONGRESS CATALOGING-IN-PUBLICATION DATA

Ferrara, Peter J., 1955–
President Obama's tax piracy / by Peter Ferrara.
p. cm. — (Encounter broadsides)
Includes bibliographical references.
ISBN-13: 978-1-59403-556-2 (pbk. : alk. paper)
ISBN-10: 1-59403-556-3 (pbk. : alk. paper)
1. Fiscal policy—United States—History—21st century.
2. Taxation—United States—History—21st century.
3. United States—Economic policy—2009– I. Title.
HJ2381.F455 2010
336.200973—dc22
2010038529

10 9 8 7 6 5 4 3 2 1